KU-345-451

S00000651926

Thundering Landslides

Louise and Richard Spilsbury

www.heinemann.co.uk/library
Visit our website to find out more information about **Heinemann Library** books.

To order:
 Phone 44 (0) 1865 888066
 Send a fax to 44 (0) 1865 314091
 Visit the Heinemann Bookshop at www.heinemann.co.uk/library to browse our catalogue and order online.

First published in Great Britain by Heinemann Library, Halley Court, Jordan Hill, Oxford OX2 8EJ, part of Harcourt Education.
Heinemann is a registered trademark of Harcourt Education Ltd.

Editorial: Andrew Farrow and Dan Nunn
Design: David Poole and Paul Myerscough
Illustrations: Geoff Ward
Picture Research: Rebecca Sodergren and Debra Weatherley
Production: Viv Hichens

Originated by Dot Gradations Limited
Printed in Hong Kong, China by Wing King Tong

ISBN 0 431 17838 0
08 07 06 05 04
10 9 8 7 6 5 4 3 2 1

British Library Cataloguing in Publication Data
Spilsbury, Richard, 1963 –
Thundering landslides. – (Awesome forces of nature)
1. Landslides – Juvenile literature
I. Title II. Spilsbury, Louise
551.3'07
A full catalogue record for this book is available from the British Library.

Acknowledgements
The publishers would like to thank the following for permission to reproduce photographs:

AFP p. **19** (Arno Balzarini); Associated Press pp. **8** (Carl Orlandi), **11** (Jun Dumaguing), **12** (Damian Dovarganes), **13** (Georg Koechler), **14** (Stefano Cardini), **15** (Maxim Marmur), **16** (Plinio Lepri), **17** (Franco Castano), **18** (Zhu Wenjie), **21** (Binod Joshi); Corbis pp. **5**, **6**, **23** (Jean Miele); Getty News and Sport pp. **20** (Devendra M. Singh), **25**; Los Angeles County Department of Public Works, Alhambra, California p. **27**; R. L. Schuster, US Geological Survey p. **26**; Rex Features pp. **4** (Sipa Press), **10** (Sipa Press), **28** (FTX); Still Pictures p. **7** (Daniel Dancer); Trip p. **24** (S. Grant); USGS p. **22**; Welsh National Assembly Photo Unit p. **9** (Crown).

Cover photograph reproduced courtesy of Rex Features/Sipa Press.

Every effort has been made to contact copyright holders of any material reproduced in this book. Any omissions will be rectified in subsequent printings if notice is given to the publishers.

Contents

*Any words appearing in the text in bold, **like this**, are explained in the Glossary.*

What is a landslide?

A landslide is when large amounts of rock, soil or mud slip down a slope. Landslides can change the Earth's surface very rapidly. They often happen without any warning. A mass of rock, soil and mud tumbling down a steep slope is heavy enough to destroy anything in its path. The force of a landslide can knock over houses and other buildings. When large amounts of mud slide down a hill they can bury whole villages below.

Landslides often pick up other things as they move. A landslide can move trees it has uprooted, cars and lorries, animals and people. The damage a landslide can cause to things in its path may be made even worse when it carries things with it.

This landslide claimed the lives of hundreds of people in this village in El Salvador within just a few minutes.

Different kinds of landslides

Landslides have different names depending on what slips. Rockfalls are when big chunks of rock break off steep slopes or cliffs and fall to the ground below. Rockslides are when differently sized chunks of rock slip down a slope. **Mudflows** are when wet soil or **debris** flows downhill as a river of mud.

Landslides come in many different sizes. A rockfall may be as small as one boulder or as big as millions of tonnes crashing down a hillside. Landslides also happen at different speeds. Soil can slip down shallow slopes at just a few metres each year, but some mudflows travel faster than a speeding car!

LANDSLIDE FACTS

! Landslides can travel at over 80 metres per second.

! Around the world, landslides injure or kill hundreds of thousands of people each year.

This landslide took place above the Indus River, in Pakistan. Tonnes of earth and rock poured into the river below.

What causes landslides?

If you put an eraser on a flat ruler it stays put. Tilt the ruler and the eraser eventually starts to slip. In the same way, rocks and soil can start to slip if a slope is too steep.

Steeper slopes

Slopes can become steeper naturally. This is often because of **erosion**. Erosion is when soil or rock is worn away. Erosion can be caused by rivers or seawater, or by wind and rain. Slopes often become steeper if the land changes shape during an **earthquake**.

Slopes can also become steeper because of things people do. Mining is when people dig up underground rocks that are useful, such as coal. When they dig, they often pile up the soil. This creates new, steeper slopes of land that can slip and slide.

When people build new roads through mountains, they sometimes cut through the mountainside and create steeper slopes.

Changing slopes

Landslides are also more likely to start if what is on a slope changes. Mountainsides naturally change over time as bits of rock break off and soil dries and crumbles. This means there is more loose **debris** on the surface. After a **volcano** has erupted, it may leave a new, heavy coating of loose **ash** on the slopes around it.

People also change hillsides. When they build houses and other buildings on slopes, they add extra weight. This extra weight means the soil and rock underneath can slip more easily. People also affect hillsides when they cut down trees. The roots of trees and other plants on slopes help hold the soil together. Without plants to help hold the soil in place, it can slide more easily.

Landslides are more likely to happen on bare slopes with few plants, like this one where trees have been cut down.

What starts a landslide?

Landslides are **triggered** (started) by many different things. The most common trigger is water. Soil, rock, ash and other **debris** can change when they get wet. They get heavier as water soaks in. They may also become slippier because little pieces slide over each other more easily. Water is more likely to trigger a landslide if a lot arrives at once. This happens in a heavy rainstorm, during a **flood** or when a lot of snow melts suddenly.

In some parts of the world, **earthquakes** can trigger landslides. Earthquakes can shake slopes so much that the rock and soil on them starts to slip. Sometimes heavy thunder can also cause landslides. Other landslides are started accidentally by people. For example, people may use explosives to blast road or railway tunnels through hillsides. This causes **vibrations** that can start a landslide.

This flooding mountain stream in Italy is washing soil and rock onto the road, preventing cars from going past.

Aberfan, Wales, UK, 1966

Aberfan is a village in Wales, in the UK. For 50 years, owners of nearby coal mines had piled up waste from the mines on hills above the village. Then, at 9:15 a.m. on 21 October 1966, thousands of tonnes of black sludge suddenly slid down towards the village below. Heavy rains, which made the coal waste very wet and heavy, **triggered** this landslide. The sludge buried 20 houses and the local primary school. Most of the 144 people who died were schoolchildren.

'It was a tremendous rumbling sound. Everyone just froze in their seats. I just managed to get up and I reached the end of my desk when the sound got louder and nearer, until I could see the black out of the window.'
Gaynor Minett, schoolchild survivor

This aerial photograph was taken shortly after the Aberfan disaster. Marked on the photograph are: 1) the village; 2) the school; 3) the coal waste; and 4) the landslide.

Where do landslides happen?

Landslides can happen all over the world, usually where there are steep slopes. The most dangerous landslides often happen at the edges of large **mountain ranges**. These include the Himalayas in Asia, the Rocky Mountains in the USA and the Andes in South America. Some mountain areas are more likely to have landslides, because they have more **gorges** (steep-sided river valleys).

Landslides also happen around coasts, especially near steep cliffs. Strong waves **erode** rocks at the bottom of the cliffs. This causes rocks to fall down from above.

Earthquake and volcano areas

Landslides are also common where there are **earthquakes** and **volcanoes**, because these things often **trigger** landslides. Earthquakes and volcanoes often happen in particular areas, such as the west coasts of North and South America, Japan and southeastern Europe.

Winter storm waves cause the worst coastal erosion.

Landslide seasons

Landslides can happen at any time of the year, but they are much more common during wet seasons. In **tropical** parts of the world, such as Central America, it is wettest in summer. The rain makes soil much heavier and rocks more slippery.

In **temperate** places, such as northern Europe, the wettest and coldest weather happens in winter and spring. When water freezes, it expands (gets bigger). When water in the cracks in rocks expands, it can break the rocks into pieces. These pieces add to the loose **debris** that slides on slopes.

LANDSLIDE FACTS

- One in three US landslides happens on slopes that have been cleared of trees.
- Clearing up landslide damage to roads costs one billion US dollars each year.

This landslide took place in Olongapo in the Philippines in July 2002. It was triggered by a week of heavy rains.

What happens in a landslide?

Landslides often happen without any warning. Sometimes, though, there are signs that can be spotted beforehand. When soil and rock begin to move before a landslide, the movement may crack water and **sewage** pipes in towns and villages. Water may bubble to the surface or damp ground may appear in places that were dry before.

There may be other signs in buildings and streets. New cracks and bulges in streets can sometimes be seen. Concrete patios and telephone poles may start to tilt. Wooden frames can twist, causing windows and doors to stick.

The next disaster

Sometimes landslides happen after other natural disasters, such as **earthquakes** or **floods.** These landslides are often worse because people are already in difficulty after the first disaster.

Sometimes, warning signs happen too late for people to get out of the way. This landslide above the Mexican village of Acalama in 1989 killed all but 30 of the 100–200 inhabitants of the village.

During a landslide

When a big landslide moves down a slope it can clear everything in its path. Landslides shift tonnes of rock and soil. Moving rocks bang into other rocks and make them move too. Small pieces of rock can act like rolling marbles, making larger pieces of rock slide more easily. As the landslide moves, it grows in size, pushing along more and more trees, rocks and other **debris**.

Tonnes of moving rocks can crush buildings, people and vehicles. Mudflows flow in and around buildings. As it dries out, the mud can set hard like concrete around anything or anyone inside. Landslides can knock down **power lines** that may injure or kill people by **electrocution**. They can also break oil and gas pipes. Leaking oil and gas can easily catch fire.

Mudflows fill spaces around buildings and cars. This often makes it very difficult to rescue people who have become trapped.

After a landslide

Even small landslides can shift the ground under buildings, forcing many to collapse. Even if a building is left standing it may not be safe. Landslides can damage the foundations of a building – foundations are the bottom bit that the rest of the building stands on. The building may then collapse without warning later on. People are also affected when landslides **pollute** water supplies. When water pipes are damaged, dirt gets inside. If people drink polluted water, they may catch diseases.

When landslides fall, they can block or break roads, railways and bridges. This makes it difficult or impossible for people to travel, even if their vehicles are undamaged. When roads are damaged, it is also more difficult for rescue workers to reach landslide victims. If falling **debris** damages telephone lines, people may not even be able to call for help.

Blocked roads like this can slow down rescue work after a major landslide.

Can landslides cause other natural disasters?

Some landslides can cause other natural disasters. One of the most common natural disasters caused by landslides is **flooding**. If mud and rock fall into rivers and streams they can make the water flow up over the sides. This is the same thing that happens when you get into a full bath – when something is added to water, its level rises. When a lot of water flows out of a river and onto land suddenly, it can flood towns and villages, and ruin farmers' fields of crops.

If a landslide splashes into water in a **fjord** (a high-sided sea valley) or harbour, it can start a giant wave. This type of wave is called a tsunami. In 1934 a cliff fell into a fjord in Norway and started a tsunami that killed hundreds of people.

This flood near Mazar-e-Sharif in northern Afghanistan in 2002 was caused by a landslide that blocked a river. More than 100 people were killed.

Sarno, Italy, 1998

The small town of Sarno sits at the bottom of a hill in southwestern Italy. Scientists had warned people living there that the area was unsafe to build on. This was because the soil on the hillside was at risk of slipping. The reasons were clear to see. Some of the hill slopes had been cleared of trees to make space for buildings. Others had been stripped bare by forest fires. In Sarno itself, many houses had been built too close to rivers. This meant that they could easily be **flooded** if water levels rose.

In early May 1998 strong rains **triggered** a massive **mudflow**. Mud and **debris** shot through the narrow streets of Sarno. When mud flowed into the river, it caused flooding. The river water made the mud thinner so it flowed even faster. Within a few minutes, the mudflow had ripped apart buildings and bridges.

> *'The force [of the mudflow] is incredible. It crushed cars as if they were Coke cans.'* Jim McConnell, a **construction engineer**

The mudflow at Sarno devastated the entire town.

Mud everywhere

The mud flowed into every part of the town. In a local hospital, it came through the windows and doors and knocked away part of the staircase. Cars and ambulances outside were left piled on top of each other like toys after a game. Roads and railway tracks were covered in piles of debris and boulders carried by the mud.

Many people were washed away or buried by the mudflow. Roberto Robustelli was eventually rescued after being trapped in a space 45 centimetres high and a metre square. He remembered:

> *'At first I thought, "Oh, I can make it, I can make it. There's enough space to breathe," but the time kept passing and I started losing hope.'*

Over 130 people died and hundreds more people were injured or made homeless by the disaster. Several thousand people could not work, go to school or live normal lives for weeks until Sarno was cleared up.

Who helps after a landslide?

People caught in landslides rely on help from others. Some help is needed urgently. For example, people trapped in buildings or under **debris** need to be rescued fast. Other help is needed during the weeks after a landslide to get life back to normal.

Fire service and police workers rescue people who are trapped and take them to safety. Ambulances and medical workers arrive as quickly as possible. They treat people who are injured, and take anyone who is seriously hurt to hospital. Workers and **volunteers** for **charities** such as the Red Cross also provide help. They set up **shelters** for rescued people to rest in until they can move on. They provide food and drink for the victims, and often for the rescue workers too.

*After a major disaster, like this in Shenzhen, China, in 2002, the scene can be very muddled and messy. Rescue workers often risk being caught in **floods** or further landslides themselves, while they work to rescue or treat people. This man is being dug out of setting mud.*

Army and Navy helicopters transport things people need. They may carry in all kinds of things, from tanks of clean drinking water to heavy lifting equipment to help clear debris. They can also fly injured people to hospital, if the landslide affected roads.

Long term

Later, **engineers** and builders move in to clear up rocks, mud and debris. They check buildings are safe and rebuild others. Many things may need to be mended or replaced. These include roads, bridges, drains, fences and **power lines**.

Illness after landslides

People's health may be affected for some time after landslides. For example, a **virus** that is blown around on dust causes a disease known as 'valley fever' in the USA. Many people caught this disease after an **earthquake** in California in 1994. The earthquake **triggered** landslides that threw lots of dust into the air.

After this landslide in Trun, Switzerland, in November 2002, engineers helped clear up the massive amounts of debris.

Nepal, 2002

In summer 2002, heavy **tropical** storms and **floods triggered** landslides in different parts of Nepal, in Asia. Many of the landslides happened in remote mountain villages that could only be reached on foot or by helicopter. It was not safe for helicopters to fly because of bad weather. Also, the Nepalese emergency services did not have enough workers or equipment to reach all the landslide sites.

The Nepal Red Cross was one of the first **charities** to help the landslide victims. The charity had a store of emergency **aid** and a large number of local, trained **volunteers**. The volunteers had to walk a long way to the villages affected by landslides.

'A vast network of volunteers made it possible for the Red Cross to work with the community immediately after the disaster. Red Cross volunteers have walked for five days to assist remote communities.' Bob McKerrow of the Red Cross

These people in Matatirtha, Nepal, are clearing mud from the spot where houses were swept away by a landslide in 2002.

Getting aid

The volunteers helped to rescue people trapped by the landslides and treated minor injuries. They contacted their headquarters and told them what people needed. Nepalese police and soldiers organized flights to take the aid to places near the affected villages. At one place, Melamchi, 32 families came to collect aid.

Nima Sherpa's family and its herd of cattle survived a landslide, but had no **shelter** against the cold mountain weather. He had never asked for help before in his life. 'It is so embarrassing to ask for help,' he said. Nima Sherpa received a family kit. The kit contained items that helped his family come through the difficult times until they could rebuild their home and get back to normal.

These Red Cross workers are preparing materials to be sent to people made homeless by landslides in Nepal. A typical rescue kit might contain items like a ***tarpaulin*** *for shelter, equipment to cook with, clothes, candles, blankets and tablets to make water clean.*

Can landslides be predicted?

Predicting landslides is not always easy. Scientists called **geologists** use lots of different information to work out whether rock and soil on a slope might slip. They then know that a landslide might be **triggered** by certain weather, such as heavy rain.

Know your slope

Geologists examine places where previous landslides happened. Landslides may happen in the same places in the future. They study rock to see how cracked it is. Rocks with cracks might break up more easily than rocks without cracks.

Scientists can use special cameras on **satellites** in space to take pictures of anywhere on Earth. This means that they can look at and study places that are difficult to get to. The pictures show whether slopes have any plants and trees on them. Bare slopes are more likely to slip than those covered with trees.

As well as using cameras on satellites, geologists also use hand-held equipment like this to study the angles of slopes.

Spotting changes

Once geologists know what slopes are like, they check them regularly to see if they are changing. Geologists compare satellite pictures to see if the slopes are getting steeper, especially those in places where many people live.

Geologists test whether the soil and rock on slopes is getting wetter. They look at weather forecasts to see how much rain or snow will fall on slopes. This extra water may trigger landslides. They also use special equipment to detect movements of the Earth. These movements can show when an **earthquake** or **volcano** is about to happen. These natural disasters can trigger landslides.

Making things worse

Prediction is more difficult when people change land. For example, when people drain land around a river to build houses, the river often floods more easily. **Flooding** can also weaken the bottoms of slopes. This means the slopes above slip more easily.

Geologists use powerful computers to help them predict landslides.

Can people prepare for landslides?

It is important to predict landslides so people can be prepared. In certain areas, landslides are a constant threat. People who live there prepare in different ways.

One way is to make slopes more **stable**. To stop rockfalls, people sometimes build strong walls at the foot of slopes. These are made of concrete blocks or wire cages filled with rocks. They also attach tough wire netting to the slope. The wire prevents rocks from falling or controls where they fall. People also plant trees on soil-covered slopes to stop the soil moving. In some places, people build strong concrete walls or channels. These direct a landslide away from towns, but can sometimes cause more damage elsewhere.

This road in Laguna Beach, California, USA, is protected from landslides by tough wire netting.

Another way to prepare for landslides is taking care over the way buildings are made. For example, if people use flexible (bendy) water and gas pipes, then ground movement during a landslide is less likely to break them. This means that the risk of **flooding** and fire after a landslide may be reduced.

Emergency plans

In areas threatened by landslides, people should know what to do in an emergency. Plans may include learning **evacuation** routes. For example, people should know how to get to the nearest safe, high ground and to never try to outrun a landslide. They should also plan where to meet up if a landslide happens when family members are in different places.

People in potential disaster areas should keep an emergency pack like the ones being prepared here. These often contain a battery-operated radio so people can hear information about the landslide. They also might contain a torch, food and clean water (or tablets to make water drinkable).

San Gabriel Mountains, California, USA

The city of Los Angeles is built at the base of the slopes of the San Gabriel Mountains in California, USA. These mountains lie on the San Andreas Fault. This is a giant crack under the surface of the Earth. The two sides of the crack push against each other. As they push, they force up the rock on top. This means the San Gabriel Mountains are getting higher. As they get higher, many parts get steeper slopes. Steeper slopes mean more landslides. As the rocks move they also cause cracks under dams and in pipes. When water spills out of these, it makes soil and rock even more likely to slide.

This photo shows the damage caused by a landslide in the town of La Conchita in southern California, in 1995. Around eleven or twelve homes were destroyed or badly damaged.

Making Los Angeles safer

Engineers in Los Angeles use different ways to try to prevent landslides in the future. One way is **debris** basins. These are shallow pits shaped a bit like football stadiums. They are built in places where landslides may happen. When the landslide passes, they catch much of the rock, soil and other debris.

There are over 100 debris basins around Los Angeles. So far, these basins have caught over 20 million tonnes of rock, soil and debris that have slid down from the San Gabriel Mountains. When a basin is full or partly full, **construction** workers use diggers and lorries to empty them. This is vital so the basins can stop future landslides. It is expensive though – it costs over 60 million US dollars each year to do this!

Here, construction workers are cleaning out a debris basin in Little Dalton, California, USA.

Can landslides be prevented?

People cannot prevent natural disasters such as landslides. The only sure way for people to avoid being affected by landslides is to live far away from slopes or hillsides, but this is not always possible. Many landslides start because of natural causes, such as **earthquakes** or heavy rain, and we cannot do anything about these.

People can prevent some landslides by being more careful about the way they use the land. For example, they should leave trees to grow on hillsides. We can also make some future landslides less damaging by carefully studying steep slopes around the world. If people know about the danger, they can be ready to escape if they have to.

A village like this should be safe from landslides. The mountain behind it is covered with thick trees that help to prevent landslides.

Major landslides of the recent past

Rio de Janeiro, Brazil, 1966
Heavy rain caused landslides from the mountain behind the city of Rio de Janeiro and killed 550 people.

Aberfan, Wales, UK, 1966
Heavy rains sent thousands of tonnes of coal waste crashing down onto the village of Aberfan from the hills above. A total of 144 people died – mostly children attending the local primary school.

Chungar, Peru, 1971
A landslide fell into Lake Yanahuani. It caused a huge wave that crashed into the nearby town of Chungar and killed more than 200 people.

Huancavelica Province, Peru, 1974
A landslide blocked a river and created a huge lake. The landslide killed over 400 people and 9000 people had to **evacuate**.

Darjeeling, India, 1980
Heavy rains set off landslides down the Himalayan slopes that killed 250 people.

Sichuan Province, China, 1981
Heavy rains triggered landslides from mountains that killed 240 people and made 100,000 people homeless.

Colombia, 1985
When the **volcano** Nevado del Ruiz erupted, it caused a **mudflow** that killed over 20,000 people.

Iran, 1990
An earthquake caused mudflows that buried whole towns and villages and killed 50,000 people.

Glossary

aid help given as money, medicine, food or other essential items
ash powder left after something burns
charity group of people who work together to raise money and to provide help for people in need
construction building or other structure, for example a bridge, road or airport
debris loose bits of solid material, such as stones and rocks
earthquake violent shaking movement of part of the Earth's surface
electrocution to injure or kill by electric shock
engineer someone who plans, designs, puts together and mends constructions
erode/erosion wearing away of rock and soil by wind, rain, water or people
evacuate/evacuation move to safety from a place of danger until that danger has passed
fjord long inlet of sea between steep-sided cliffs
flood when a normally dry area of land is covered by water
geologist scientist who studies rocks and the way the rocks of the Earth formed
gorge steep-sided river valley
mountain range row of mountains of similar age
mudflow when wet soil or debris flows downhill as a river of mud
pollute poison or harm any part of the water, land or air in the world around us
power lines main electricity cables
satellite special machine in space that travels around above the Earth and can take photographs
sewage waste matter, such as excrement (poo), that is carried in sewers
shelter safe place protected from rain, cold and other dangers
stable fixed and not easily moved
tarpaulin waterproof sheet or cloth
temperate climate that is warm and dry in summer and wet and mild in winter
trigger/triggered cause/caused
tropical area near the equator that is hot all year round
vibration shaking to and fro
virus tiny living thing that can cause disease in plants and animals
volcano opening in the Earth's surface through which hot liquid rock and gases can escape
volunteer person who offers help without being paid

Find out more

Books

Avalanches and Landslides, J. Walker (Franklin Watts, 2002)

Landslides and Avalanches, Terry Jennings (Belitha Press, 1999)

Landslides, Slumps, and Creep (First Books – Earth & Sky Science), Pete H. Goodwin (Franklin Watts, 1998)

Websites

www.fema.gov/hazards/landslides – the US Federal Emergency Management Agency (FEMA) website has a useful fact sheet about landslides and mudflow.

http://landslides.usgs.gov/html_files/nlicsun.html – the website of the US National Landslide Information Center is a good place to find out more about recent landslides around the world.

Index

Titles in the *Awesome Forces of Nature* series include:

Hardback 0 431 17828 3

Hardback 0 431 17831 3

Hardback 0 431 17829 1

Hardback 0 431 17835 6

Hardback 0 431 17830 5

Hardback 0 431 17836 4

Hardback 0 431 17832 1

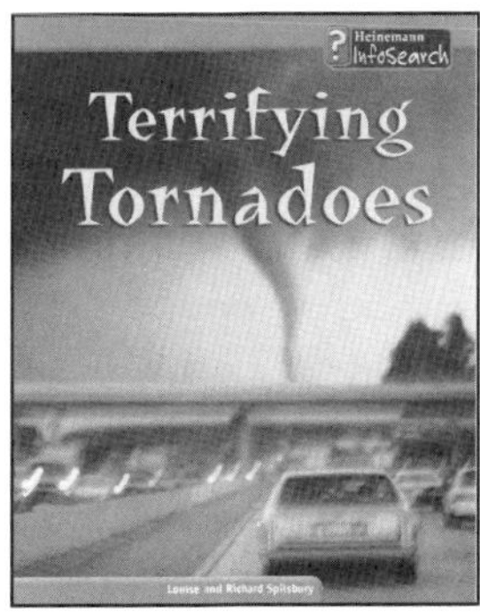

Hardback 0 431 17837 2

Hardback 0 431 17838 0

Hardback 0 431 17834 8

Find out about the other titles in this series on our website
www.heinemann.co.uk/library